Doctor Crispin

Noël Le Breton de Hauteroche

Translated
with an introduction by
Edwin L. Isley

Seventeenth-century Press

ISBN-10: 0692235507
ISBN-13: 978-0692235508

For my beautiful wife for her love and support.

Preface to *Doctor Crispin* (1670) by Noël Le Breton,
sieur de Hauteroche

Noël Le Breton, known as Hauteroche, had an illustrious career in the theatre as an actor, administrator, and a playwright. It was he who provided, from the company of four actor-playwrights--including Poisson, Brécourt, and Champmeslé--the greatest number of new plays for the theatre of the Hôtel de Bourgogne, the theatre that was to become the chief rival of Molière and his company. Very few playwrights have had such contemporary admiration and such a loyal following as Hauteroche.

Doctor Crispin, a three-acter written in prose, appeared in 1670. This is by far Hauteroche's most popular play with well over eight-hundred performances at the Comédie-Française alone.

The fact that this play was performed well into the nineteenth century serves as a testament not only to its general success but also to its craftsmanship.

The stock character Crispin had a rich stage life of sixty years as one of the most popular and important figures of dramatic comedy from the mid-seventeenth century to the early eighteenth century. In 1654, Paul Scarron (1610?-1660) wrote *L'Écolier de Salamanque ou les généreux ennemis*, tragédie-comédie, five acts in verse, in which he introduced the famous character. He drew the subject matter of his play from the Spanish playwright Francisco de Rojas Zorrilla's *Obligados y ofendidos* (1641). The valet's name was Crispinillo; Scarron gallicizes the name of the servant but leaves intact the features of his character" (Curtis, p. 80).

Noël Le Breton de Hauteroche

In *Doctor Crispin*, the witty valet, whose well-meant efforts land him in serious trouble, is the central figure who contributes much to the development and the conclusion of the play. Although he is far from brave, Crispin literarily risks life and limbs for the union of the lovers. He appears in over half of the scenes, and, especially, when dressed as a doctor, is in complete command of the stage. Most critics, including myself, believe that the huge success of the play is due in great part to the so-called "dissection scene" (II, iii). Crispin, stretched out on a table, ready to be dissected alive, and shaking with fear, always brings roars of laughter from the audience (LaPorte, pp. 222-223).

One of the most rewarding and profitable schemes to which the comic doctor resorted was his display of a medical hocus-pocus of Greek, Latin, Arabic, and other "unknown" languages for the purpose of confusing the naïve patient. The custom of using Latin was very common, not only the educated doctor but even the "physician despite himself" could spout enough Latin to conceal his faults and to extricate himself from difficult situations. Hauteroche attacks doctors as fakes and ignorant men, who disguise their lack of knowledge under a veneer of learned words. Crispin's "… Araca, lostovi, baritonovaï…" rivals the false Latinism found in Molière's finest doctor comedies. While Crispin is obviously meant to parody the poor preparation of doctors, his situation is not so extreme. An ignorant man pretending to be a physician is not really any more dangerous than the fraudulent doctor with antiquated knowledge trying to cheat people, who are ill, out of their money.

Edwin L. Isley

DOCTOR CRISPIN,
COMEDY.

CHARACTERS.

LISIDOR, Geralde's Father.

GERALDE, Alcine's Suitor.

MIROBOLAN, Physician, Alcine's Father.

FELIANTE, Alcine's Mother.

ALCINE.

DORINE, Feliante's Servant.

MARIN, Lisidor's Valet.

CRISPIN, Geralde's Valet.

LISE, Servant.

A SURGEON.

GRAND-SIMON.

The Scene is in Paris.[1]

---

[1] Hauteroche provides little information about the setting of the play: "La scène est à Paris." "The place includes a street before a house and two apartments within it, as shown by the requirements indicated in the *Le Mémoire de Mahelot* (p. 137). The first apartment, belonging to old Lisidor must be luxuriously decorated, indicating the wealth accumulated from a long and prosperous life. The other house shows Doctor Mirobolan's surgery, which has an entrance from the outside, an interior door, and another door leading to the *cave*. There are several tools of the medical professions present, including nails, ropes, a saw, and viols of pills.

DOCTOR CRISPIN,[2]

COMEDY.

ACT I.

FIRST SCENE.

LISIDOR, MARIN.

MARIN.

What, sir! You say that you want to get remarried?

LISIDOR.

Yes, yes, I want to get remarried, and to do so, I have sent my son to Bourges[3] under the pretext of spending some time studying jurisprudence.

MARIN.

Alright, but may I ask you the name of whom you want to marry?

---

[2] Paul Scarron, in 1654, created the stock character Crispin in his comedy *L'Écolier de Salamanque.*

[3] Bourges is a small town located at the eastern end of the Loire Valley, approximately 120 miles (95 kilometers) from Paris.

LISIDOR.

It is Alcine.

MARIN.

What! Dr. Mirobolan's daughter?

LISIDOR.

Yes.

MARIN.

You're kidding, sir? That girl's not more than eighteen years old and would be more appropriate for your son than for you.

LISIDOR.

I do not want my son to get married for three or four years.

MARIN.

But, sir, have you thought about what you're doing when you consider this plan to marry Alcine?

LISIDOR.

What! Have I thought about it? Yes, yes I have thought about it a great deal. She is beautiful. She is sensible. She is young. She is witty. Moreover, she has many extraordinary qualities.

MARIN.

Well, those are all beautiful qualities which should stop you from thinking about it because to tell the truth, they're hardly appropriate for an old man.

LISIDOR.

Well, I am not that old!

MARIN.

No! Not if we were in the time when men lived seven or eight hundred years, you'd be only a young adolescent, but the time in which we live, I think that you're heading towards the end of the line.

LISIDOR.

But, sixty years old…

MARIN.

My word, not to lie about it, I believe that you're at least twelve or fourteen years older than that because I remember the other day good ol' Pyrante, having a little drink with you, said that he was more than sixty-six years old, that you were in philosophy class, and that he was in only sixth grade, and that in the school play he played Cupid[4] while you played the Emperor.

---

[4] Cupid is the Roman god of love, identified with the Greek Eros. He is always depicted as a child.

LISIDOR.

He does not know what he is talking about; he is one of those people who like to pretend that he is older than he is.

MARIN.

Let's leave age out of it, for, as they say, it's only grey hair, sir. But, let's talk a little about your marriage. Do you believe that Dr. Mirobolan and Feliante, his wife, will give you their daughter's hand, having only the one daughter? When people have an only daughter, and marry her off, it's in the hope that they'll see her have children. But, keeping nothing from you, if you marry her, they run the great risk of never having that joy, at least not without some assistance... if you see my point.

LISIDOR.

This is none of your business, and I know very well what I am doing. When she is my wife, we will do whatever has to be done.

MARIN.

My word, I doubt that she'll ever be your wife.

LISIDOR.

And me, I am certain of it. Dr. Mirobolan is a man of his word; he has promised her to me.

MARIN.

That's something, but, you know that Feliante's a
domineering woman, and, if I'm not mistaken, she seems
to wear the pants in the family.

LISIDOR.

I know that she is a little proud, but the advantages that I
will bring to her daughter will soften her pride.
Furthermore, a husband is always the master of his wife.

MARIN.

Always? My word, I've seen many people who don't live in
harmony and who'd wish with all their heart that what
you're saying were true. But sir, there's Mirobolan coming
out of his house.

SCENE II.

MIROBOLAN, LISIDOR, MARIN.

MIROBOLAN.

Ah! So it is you Mr. Lisidor.

LISIDOR.

At your service. I have come to speak about this business.

MIROBOLAN.

About what business?

LISIDOR.

Oh, the one that you know about.

MIROBOLAN.

What?

LISIDOR.

The business about which we spoke.

MIROBOLAN.

When?

LISIDOR.

On several occasions.

MIROBOLAN.

Where?

LISIDOR.

In various places.

MIROBOLAN.

I do not know what it is.

LISIDOR.

It is about your daughter's marrying me.

MIROBOLAN.

Oh, it is only that! I thought that it was about something else. Concerning that, you know that I have given you my word; you have only to choose the day, and rest assured that you are in charge of that business.

LISIDOR.

I am much obliged, but have you had the opportunity to talk about it with your better half?

MIROBOLAN.

No, but I give you her consent. She is submissive to our will. What is more, I know how to settle her down if she makes things difficult. I am the master, once and for all, and we know, thank God, how to bring a little reason to a woman.

LISIDOR.

I do not doubt it at all.

MIROBOLAN.

I would like to see her get huffy with me, and if she were to go against my resolve, I will make her see just how stupid she is. But thank Heaven, I do not have to, and my wife, in a word, does everything that I wish.

LISIDOR.

Decide, please, which one of us will talk to her about it first. It is social courtesy which I would like to observe, and you know how women are jealous of their little prerogatives.

MIROBOLAN.

Oh gladly, and, in fact, I am going to have her come here.

(*He[5] enters.*)

LISIDOR.

Well Marin, what do you have to say about that?

MARIN.

Everything's going very well, and I'm comforted by your father-in-law.

---

[5] At first, it is unclear as to whom Hauteroche is referring. It is Marin who enters.

SCENE III.

MIROBOLAN, FELIANTE, LISIDOR, MARIN.

MIROBOLAN.

My wife, here is our good friend Mr. Lisidor.

FELIANTE.

Ah, I am his servant,[6] and I am delighted to see him.

MIROBOLAN *whispering to Lisidor.*

Speak first! It will be more tactful.

LISIDOR *whispering.*

It is up to you to start, and then I will follow up.

MIROBOLAN *whispering.*

You can explain it better than I.

LISIDOR *whispering.*

Not at all. Besides, reason dictates that you broach the subject.

---

[6] Feliante is figuratively expressing her reverence for Mr. Lisidor.

MIROBOLAN *whispering*.

It is up to you to take the first step.

LISIDOR *whispering*.

I have done it with you, and you must predispose her before I speak to her.

FELIANTE.

At least, tell me what you are bickering about and the reason you had me come here.

LISIDOR.

Madam, it is a small matter.

MIROBOLAN.

My wife, it is our friend Mr. Lisidor, who is asking for our daughter's hand in marriage.

FELIANTE.

And for whom?

LISIDOR.

For myself, madam, but under conditions which cannot be unpleasant to you. Perhaps at first my age will put you off about this marriage, but madam, when you understand the great advantages that I bring to her without your spending a penny and that your husband has given me his word, I dare to hope that you will be as kind.

FELIANTE.

All of these things are very important, but your age, sir, does not match my daughter's at all, and we often see young women in such marriages fall into debauchery. The caresses of an old man in marriage are not meant for a young person; they will bring about a lot of antipathy, we even see nature revolt against it. Thus, sir, to avoid the disgraces which could befall my family, you will understand why I refuse to give you my consent.

LISIDOR.

But, madam, your husband has given me his word.

FELIANTE.

I believe it, but apparently, he has not given it much thought because if he had, he would undoubtedly share my opinion.

LISIDOR.

Sir, you know that you promised me.

FELIANTE.

I believe, once again, that he promised her to you, but he can take back his promise to you because, obviously, it will not happen.

LISIDOR.

Sir, an honorable man must keep his word. Speak! Did you not promise me your daughter's hand in marriage?

MIROBOLAN.

Oh... all of that is true.

FELIANTE.

Well, if he promised her to you, I did not! And that is enough.

MIROBOLAN.

My wife... .

FELIANTE.

Oh, my God, let me speak! I know very well what I am doing.

MIROBOLAN.

But it is necessary...

FELIANTE.

It is necessary not to make promises so easily. Once again, it will never happen, and your arguments could not be worse than they are. Goodbye, sir! Get it in your head that you will never have my daughter.

SCENE IV.

LISIDOR, MIROBOLAN, MARIN.

MARIN *to Mirobolan.*

Sir?

MIROBOLAN.

What do you want?

MARIN.

I am the master, once and for all, and we know, thank God, how to bring a little reason to a woman. I would like to see her to get huffy with me, and if she were to go against my resolve, I will make her see just how stupid she is. But, thank Heaven, I do not have to, and my wife, in a word, does everything that I wish.[7]

LISIDOR.

Actually, Marin is right, and that is the speech that you made to me before we spoke to your wife.

---

[7] Although Marin was off stage, he was obviously close enough to overhear Mirobolan in order to be able to paraphrase him so accurately.

MIROBOLAN.

That is true, but it is necessary to be a little bit patient. It is not necessary to get carried away right from the get go. One should bring some temperance to things. I give you my word, okay.... . Go on! Leave it to me.

MARIN.

Okay, leave it to the gentleman. He'll ruin everything. My word, you'd better believe the words of the wife than those of the husband. You can clearly see that she alone is the master and the mistress.

MIROBOLAN.

You do not know what you are saying.

MARIN.

No, but I know that you were just shot half way to the moon. Tell me, please, who do you think is the master, you or your wife?

MIROBOLAN.

I am.

MARIN.

Yes, in words, but not in deeds.

MIROBOLAN.

Understand that I am in fact and even in words. You are a fool!

MARIN.

Ah, sir! I'm not disputing that quality with you.

MIROBOLAN.

Shut up! (*to Lisidor.*) Sir, once again…. . Enough, goodbye.

SCENE V.

LISIDOR, MARIN.

MARIN.

The devil that was well said, sir! You mustn't hope to marry Miss Alcine because this opinionated and imperious mother will never give her to you. As for the husband, he's a skilled doctor, a great astrologer, and a great psychic,[8] but in his house he's not always the master. Therefore, you mustn't count on his promises.

---

[8] Being an astrologer, a person who studies of the position and aspect of heavenly bodies with a view to predicting their influence on the course of human affairs, and a psychic, a person who is capable of perceiving extrasensory and nonphysical mental processes, was often highly revered in seventeenth-century France.

LISIDOR.

But, do I not see Crispin?

MARIN.

Yes, sir, it's he.

SCENE VI.

CRISPIN, LISIDOR, MARIN.

CRISPIN.

Ah, sir, at your service! Good day, Marin.

MARIN.

Good day.

LISIDOR.

What brings you to this town?

CRISPIN.

It's your son, who sent me here by stagecoach. Thus it took only a week for me to come from Bourges to Paris.

MARIN.

Stagecoaches are expensive. You should've been sent on foot.

LISIDOR.

Why did he send you?

CRISPIN.

Sir, here's a letter that'll tell you everything.

LISIDOR *reading.*

My Father, I'm found down and out, I thank God for you. Another thing not to ask you, otherwise I beg of you…

This is neither my son's style nor his handwriting. Are you trying to pull my leg?

CRISPIN.

No, sir! I ask your pardon. You see, I lost my master's letter on the way, and I had this one written by a village peasant, but, anyway, I know that he was asking for money and that he was telling you that his clothes have turned to rags. Read the rest of the letter.

LISIDOR.

Huh, I am satisfied with what I have read.

MARIN.

Is it you who dictated it to the peasant?

CRISPIN.

Yes, I did! What's your point?

MARIN.

Nothing, other than it's well contrived.

CRISPIN.

You're always the wonderful speaker, and the great wit, but, by damn, figure out that I'm smarter than you.

MARIN.

Ha, I don't doubt it.

CRISPIN.

Damn! Do you want a fist fight? You'll see if... .

LISIDOR.

Will the two of you shut up!

CRISPIN.

But, sir, he always acts like he knows everything and believes that no one's as smart as he.

MARIN.

Oh! I defer to you.

LISIDOR.

Once again, shut up! But Crispin, has he has used up all of his money and his clothes in four months as you say?

CRISPIN.

Yes, sir, if it weren't true, I wouldn't tell you so.

LISIDOR.

It has been used up rather quickly. But, go home, and get some rest. I will talk to you later. I have, at the moment, some pressing business. Let's go. Follow me, Marin.

SCENE VII.

CRISPIN

CRISPIN.

Of course, he puts up that front. He's the only one who knows anything. Damn, when he gets that attitude, you'd think that no one was as smart as he, let alone smarter. But let's go to ol' Lisidor's house to get the money. My master needs it; the money that he spends every day…. But I see him, I mustn't tell him that I lost the letter, he could beat me.

SCENE VIII.

GERALDE, CRISPIN

GERALDE.

Tell me, what are you doing here?

CRISPIN.

Nothing, sir.

GERALDE.

What? I left you two hours ago. You have not been to my father's yet?

CRISPIN.

No, sir, but I met him in the street, and our business has been taken care of.

GERALDE.

How?

CRISPIN.

I gave him your letter, and told him about you needing money, in a word, what you needed.

GERALDE.

And what did he say to you?

CRISPIN.

Nothing, other than that I go and wait for him at the house and that he'd speak to me later, and that, for the moment, he's gone to town on some business.

GERALDE.

Did he not ask you about my behavior?

CRISPIN.

Not much, but I expect that he will soon, and that's why I must wait on him.

GERALDE.

Be careful, at least... .

CRISPIN.

Well, leave it to me! We're not as stupid as we are badly dressed. He believes all my nonsense.

GERALDE.

Watch out especially for Marin. As you know, he is trouble.

CRISPIN.

I don't care about him. Damn, just because he knows how to read and write, and I don't know how to at all, he thinks we're not as smart as he. I thought about socking him one.

GERALDE.

So he was with my father?

CRISPIN.

Yes, and already wanted to argue, but we've set him back. Go, rely on me: you know that I'm not a great talker, but I get the things done that you ask of me. Where are you coming from?

GERALDE.

Alcine told me that she had something that she wanted me to know and that I would find her somewhere in back of the house…. But I believe that I see her now.

SCENE IX.

ALCINE, DORINE, GERALDE, CRISPIN

ALCINE.

Geralde, you have come too early. I asked you to come two hours later.

GERALDE.

You are right, miss, but you know the impatience that
routinely torments lovers, and how they believe that their
pains are eased when they can see the place where they will
meet the person whom they love.

ALCINE.

Geralde, stop with the kind flattery because I cannot stay
long with you! I am going to meet my mother. You must
know only that your father wants to marry me.

GERALDE.

My father?

ALCINE.

Yes, your father, and mine has given him his word, but my
mother, as you know, is the master of the household and
has rebuffed the good man Lisidor. Now, you see the
quandary before us. It will take time to reveal to her the
love that I have for you and to get her to be favorable to
my wishes. Your father will not consent. Furthermore, we
must hope for nothing from my mother without your
father's consent. Goodbye! I am afraid that she is coming
right behind me.

Crispin and Dorine exchange great bows to each other.

SCENE X.

GERALDE, CRISPIN

GERALDE.

What should I do now, dear Crispin?

CRISPIN.

What's driving that old geezer to fall in love at the age of seventy-four? No doubt that's why he sent us to Bourges, but we have to prevent him from marrying her. With only some money, we can cut him out of the picture. Look at the old coot! He needs eighteen-year-old girls to make him happy! He's not completely disgusting: he does rather well! He just needs a conk on the head.

GERALDE.

But what to do, Crispin?

CRISPIN.

Try to speak to her alone, and, with that, you'll resolve all of the issues. She'll give you the possible means.... .

GERALDE.

Come, I am going to write her a letter that you will deliver to Dorine once they have returned home.

CRISPIN.

But, I must go to your father's house.

GERALDE.

Nonetheless, I want you to take my letter before going there.

End of the first Act.

Doctor Crispin

ACT II.

FIRST SCENE.

MIROBOLAN, DORINE

MIROBOLAN.

Dorine, Dorine? Hey, Dorine?

DORINE *entering*.

Sir?

MIROBOLAN.

Prepare this room properly in order to receive those who will do me the honor of attending the autopsy[9] that I will perform on the cadaver that the public executioner is sending me.

DORINE.

But, sir, why choose this apartment? All of the other times, you did it in the other house.

---

[9] Autopsies were usually unsanctioned and illegal in seventeenth-century France.

MIROBOLAN.

That is true. But my wife wanted me to make use of the house in the back so that the main house would be freed up; I think that she has a good point.

DORINE.

Ah! I don't doubt it.

MIROBOLAN.

Now that we are in a separate place, the garden that separates these two houses will hush the noise that the opinionated ordinarily make on such occasions. There is always somebody who does not agree with the others and who points out an erroneous opinion, and makes more noise than four.

DORINE.

In all truth, sir, even though you're all doctors, you can hardly agree. Your science is very uncertain, and you're the first to be mistaken.

MIROBOLAN.

That happens sometimes, but that is not the fault of medicine.

DORINE.

It must, therefore, be the doctors' fault since it's not the fault of medicine.

MIROBOLAN.

That might be true, but Dorine, that is not your business.

DORINE.

No, but I can speak my mind, and if it's not my business today, it'll be someday despite me.

MIROBOLAN.

Very good, but let's change the subject, and think about receiving the cadaver that should be arriving very soon. Have it put in the cellar because I will not start work until tomorrow. Now, I am going to see three or four patients for whom I do not have much hope.

DORINE.

I'll do all that you ask.

MIROBOLAN *returning*.

If Dorine wanted to do all that I ask of her, she could show me a little tenderness, and she would certainly not be angry at all.

DORINE.

Should you have such thoughts, having a wife as fine as yours? It seems to me that that's not reasonable, and you ought to be happy with her.

MIROBOLAN.

It is a strange thing to be obliged to eat only bread, one gets bored in the end.

DORINE.

If madam, your wife, wanted the same thing, what would you say?

MIROBOLAN.

Oh! That is not the same thing. Man's glory is to cajole several women, but woman's virtue is to listen to only her husband.

DORINE.

I don't believe in men having more privileges than women and men being permitted to do what women dare not undertake.

MIROBOLAN.

The law wants it be this way.

DORINE.

In fact, it should be just the opposite. Those who established that law were ignorant, for there are as many ignorant lawyers as there are ignorant doctors. But, I see that you have many to give to me. I'm sure that you'd have a hard time showing me that law. Go see your patients, and leave me in peace.

MIROBOLAN.

No goodbyes, Dorine?

SCENE II.

DORINE.

DORINE.

No goodbyes, sir. See the jolly ol' fellow! There's nothing to do but to leave him alone, and he'll do some wonderful things. It's a strange thing when these despicable men can't content themselves with their wives, they have to have find new women. If I'm ever married, and my husband plays such games, what's good for the goose is good for the gander, we'll see.... Ah Crispin! What do you want?

SCENE III.

CRISPIN, DORINE

CRISPIN.

I was hanging around here, to see if I could give you this letter. I saw Dr. Mirobolan leave, and, at the same time, I came in, as you see.

DORINE.

Close that door so we can speak without being overheard. I'm going to close this one. *(They each close a door.)* Well, who sent this letter?

CRISPIN.

My master who's becoming desperate because Alcine told him something concerning her marriage to his father.

DORINE.

We'll have to prevent that.

CRISPIN.

By Jove, you'd lose more than one person. You'd not have the advantage of having me for a husband, me who loves you more than fifty men.

DORINE.

You believe that's a great advantage?

CRISPIN.

Without a doubt! But, let's not dwell on that anymore, the gentleman deserves the lady, and the lady deserves the gentleman. Tell me, what were you doing in here with Mr. Mirobolan?

DORINE.

He has to perform the dissection of a hanged man tomorrow, and since he's chosen this place to do it, he ordered me to get it ready as soon as possible. Now, it's necessary for your master to make special arrangements to speak to our lady. Since this place is going to be occupied, they'll no longer have the liberty to meet here as easily as they used to. Give this letter to me, I'll find the opportunity to give it to Alcine and get a reply.

CRISPIN.

Here, go quickly.

SCENE IV.

MIROBOLAN, FELIANTE, DORINE, CRISPIN

MIROBOLAN *knocking on the door from the street entrance.*

Hey, hey, Dorine? Open up for me right away.

DORINE.

My God, what am I going to do? It's our master.

CRISPIN.

Ah! damn it, I'd like to be far from here.

FELIANTE *knocking at the other door.*

Oh, Dorine! Open the door for me.

DORINE.

Ah, this is getting worse! It's our mistress.

CRISPIN.

Hey, it's the devil.

DORINE.

Without her, I was going to put you in the cellar.

MIROBOLAN *knocking again.*

Come on! Open the door for me, Dorine.

DORINE.

I'm at a loss.

CRISPIN.

I am too.

DORINE.

Crispin, spread out on this table. I'll say you're the hanged man that they've just dropped off.

CRISPIN.

But... .

DORINE.

Don't argue! Do what I tell you.

Crispin lies on the table, and Dorine opens the door for Mirobolan.

MIROBOLAN *entering quickly.*

You made me wait a long time. I forgot something upstairs that I have to get right away.

He exits via a door near the one by which Feliante enters. Dorine now opens the door for Feliante.

FELIANTE.

Where were you when I was calling you?

DORINE.

I was busy receiving this cadaver, and I heard you only just now.

MIROBOLAN *reentering.*

My wife, what are you doing here?

FELIANTE.

I came to see if Dorine has prepared the room as she was supposed to.

MIROBOLAN *leaving.*

See you later. See you later.

FELIANTE.

Dorine, take care of everything here! As for me, I am leaving right away because I do not like to see such objects. They always give me depressing thoughts.

DORINE.

Go, go, madam, I'll do everything that's necessary. Well, Crispin, did my little plan work or not?

She recloses the doors.

CRISPIN.

Very well, and we got out of it cheaply, but I'm leaving soon to avoid any new trouble. Perhaps if I stayed longer... .

MIROBOLAN *returning.*

Dorine, Dorine? Open the door! Open the door for me.

DORINE.

Ah! Get back in the same position right away. It's our doctor once again.

CRISPIN *getting back on the table.*

The devil take him away.

Dorine reopens the door.

MIROBOLAN *entering*.

I think that I am not in my right mind today. I have forgotten half of the things I need, certain pills that I promised.... But what do I see there, Dorine?

DORINE.

It's the cadaver that they've just brought. He was already here when you came before.

MIROBOLAN.

Very good! But why does he still have his clothes on?

DORINE.

They said that they'd come and get them later.

MIROBOLAN *touching him*.

There is nothing missing. I am of the opinion that since he is still warm that I will begin the dissection. Go fetch my lancets which are up in my cabinet.

DORINE.

But, sir, you have nothing prepared. It'd be too much trouble, and besides your patients are waiting for you.

MIROBOLAN.

Waiting two or three hours, there's no great harm.

DORINE.

But what if someone dies?

MIROBOLAN.

That would not be my fault because if he dies in such a short time, my visit would not help him very much.

DORINE.

But a timely remedy… .

MIROBOLAN.

Just go, and bring me a package of twine and some nails that you will find right by the lancets. While he is still warm, I will find the lacteal veins[10] and the reservoirs which conduct the chlye[11] to the heart during sanguification[12] more easily.

DORINE.

But, sir, you're going to take away my privilege of preparing this place, as I want it. Wait until tomorrow, as you said.

---

[10] The lacteal veins are lymphatic capillaries that absorb dietary fat in the small intestine.

[11] Chlye is a milky, bodily fluid that contains lymphatic fluid.

[12] Sanguification is the production of blood.

MIROBOLAN.

Either go, or I will go myself.

DORINE.

I'll go since you insist.

MIROBOLAN *looking at him.*

He does not look malevolent, but there is something inauspicious about his face. Yes, all of the rules of metoposcopy[13] and physiognomy[14] are false if he did not deserve to be hanged. (*He unbuttons him*) Ah! what pleasure I am going to take making a primary incision on his body and to open him up from his xyphoid cartilage[15] right down to his pubis.[16] His heart is still beating! Ah if my

---

[13] Metoposcopy is the art of judging human character from the features of the forehead.

[14] Physiognomy is the art of judging human character from facial features.

[15] The xyphoid cartilage refers to the smallest of the three divisions of the sternum.

[16] The pubis is the forward portion either of the hipbones, at the juncture forming the front arch of the pelvis.

MIROBOLAN (continued)

colleagues were here now, particularly the erroneous ones, I would make them see, by his systole[17] and diastole,[18] the circulation of the blood.

SCENE V.

A SURGEON, MIROBOLAN

THE SURGEON *entering by the door that Mirobolan left open.*

Sir, the baron has been extremely bloated since yesterday, and you must go see him as soon as possible.

MIROBOLAN.

I will go soon. I do not have the luxury at the moment.

THE SURGEON.

But the illness is urgent, sir. It is necessary that you come now.

---

[17] Systole is the rhythmic contraction of the heart, especially to the ventricles, by which blood is driven through the aorta and the pulmonary artery.

[18] Diastole is the rhythmically occurring relaxation and dilation of the heart during which the cavities are filled with blood.

MIROBOLAN.

I cannot; go, bleed him as usual. I will see him in two hours.

THE SURGEON.

Sir, I do not believe that bleeding will do him any good.

MIROBOLAN.

Bleed him. I tell you. I know what I am doing.

THE SURGEON.

But, sir… .

MIROBOLAN.

But once again, bleed him.

THE SURGEON.

But, sir… .

MIROBOLAN.

But I want him bled. What business do surgeons have arguing with doctors?

THE SURGEON.

Sir, I will not bleed him at all because I am convinced that the slightest bleeding is capable of causing his death.

MIROBOLAN.

He will be, despite you, and I will have him bled by someone else.

THE SURGEON.

You will do as you please. As for me, I will not do it. Goodbye!

MIROBOLAN.

Goodbye!

SCENE VI.

DORINE, CRISPIN, MIROBOLAN

DORINE *having heard.*

I don't know where to find all of your tools, and besides madam's told me to inform you that you're urgently needed at the baron's.

MIROBOLAN *leaving.*

It will have to put it off until tomorrow. Dorine, have this cadaver placed in the cellar.

DORINE *closing the door after him.*

Go! I'll take care of everything.

CRISPIN *getting up.*

And me, without entertaining any arguments, I'm leaving immediately.

DORINE.

Where are you going?

CRISPIN.

What the hell! Where do I want to go? Let me leave. What! You coldly look for the lancets, and all of those instruments to carve me into pieces, and you want me to stay? You're kidding.

DORINE.

Understand that when I left to look for the tools, it was with the intention of hiding them where he'd never find them, and that's what I did.

CRISPIN.

Oh, that was well done. At first I was astonished, me your future husband, that you had the composure to see me cut up so barbarically.

DORINE.

I wouldn't have ever allowed it. But, wait for me here, I'm going to try to deliver this letter, and get a reply.

CRISPIN.

I don't want to wait in this place.

DORINE.

Why not?

CRISPIN.

The word lancet makes me shake. I'm going to wait for you in the street. There I don't fear Dr. Lancets. As for me, it seems, from the fear that I had, that this room is completely filled with them.

DORINE.

Go, but don't be impatient.

CRISPIN.

I'll gladly wait, once I'm out of here.

As he is leaving, someone knocks on door.

Ah! Here's the devil once again! As soon as you open the door, I'm running out.

DORINE.

Don't do it! You'd ruin everything. Lie down again quickly.

CRISPIN.

I'll do nothing of the kind, anything could happen. What if he had some lancets in his pocket… .

DORINE.

If I'd not forgotten the key to the cellar, I'd put you in there.

CRISPIN.

Do what you want, but I'm not getting back up there anymore.

DORINE.

Listen, I'm going to bring you down a doctor's robe, you'll say that you learned that he was going to perform a dissection, you came to pay him a visit. As for the hanged man, I'll say that I had him put in the cellar.

More knocking on the door.

CRISPIN.

Go, I much prefer to play a doctor than a hanged man. By God, wait, if you want, let me get dressed! At least in these clothes, I run no risk of being sliced open or being beaten. When I appear ignorant, well there're plenty of other doctors who are just as ignorant.

DORINE *returning.*

Hey, put it on so I can open the door.

CRISPIN *having put on the robe.*

Here I am, very debonair.

SCENE VII.

LISE, CRISPIN, DORINE *having opened the door.*

LISE.

Is the Doctor in?

DORINE.

No.

LISE.

There he is. Why hide him from me?

DORINE.

What do you want from him?

LISE.

Just to say a couple of words to him.

CRISPIN *gravely.*

What do you want from me?

LISE.

Sir, you know, my mistress has lost a puppy that she loves madly, to the point of despair, and she blames it all on me. Anyway, I'm told that that you're an astrologer as well as a doctor?

CRISPIN.

I am as knowledgeable in one as the other.

LISE.

That's what brought me here, to beg you, to pay you, to give me some news about it.

CRISPIN.

How long has it been lost?

LISE.

Two days.

CRISPIN.

At what time?

LISE.

Around eleven o'clock in the morning.

CRISPIN.

What color is its fur?

LISE.

White and black.

CRISPIN *seeming in a dream-like state.*

That suffices.

LISE *to Dorine.*

Oh, the wonderful man! He's going to give us news about our puppy.

DORINE.

No doubt.

CRISPIN.

Listen. Two days ago?

LISE.

Yes, sir.

CRISPIN.

Around eleven o'clock.

LISE.

Yes.

CRISPIN.

Black and white?

LISE.

Yes.

CRISPIN.

Take some pills.[19]

LISE.

Some pills?

CRISPIN.

Yes.

LISE.

But will that find the dog?

CRISPIN.

Yes.

LISE.

But still, what kind of pills?

CRISPIN.

The very freshest from the pharmacy.

LISE.

But, sir…

---

[19] Pills, in this case, refer to laxatives.

CRISPIN.

But don't argue so much! Do exactly as I say.

LISE.

How many should I take?

CRISPIN.

Three. LISE *giving him a silver coin.*[20]

That's enough. If I find my dog this way, I'll send you a lot of clients.

CRISPIN.

If you don't find it, it'll not be the fault of the remedy.

LISE.

I believe you. Goodbye, sir!

CRISPIN.

Goodbye.

DORINE *after having shut the door.*

Well, Crispin, you had just put on the doctor's robe, and you received a piece of silver.

---

[20] The silver and gold coins used in seventeenth-century France were the *écu.* An *écu* derives its name from the old French meaning shield. A shield was stamped on the coin.

CRISPIN.

By Jove! I see that this is a good profession. Without knowing what one's doing, one earns money, and without running the risk of playing the hanged man.

DORINE.

I could hardly stop myself from laughing at your prescription. Pills to find a lost dog!

CRISPIN.

What the heck do you want me to prescribe? Me who doesn't know how to read or write, or know anything that she expects me to know. The pills came to mind, so I prescribed them. I'm taking off this robe and waiting in the street, as we said.

More knocking.

DORINE.

Someone's knocking on the door. Put it back on.

CRISPIN.

Again! I fear it may be your master.

DORINE *going to open the door.*

What does it matter? We'll pull the wool over his eyes.

SCENE VIII.

GRAND-SIMON, DORINE, CRISPIN

GRAND-SIMON.

Is Dr. Mirobolan here?

DORINE.

Why?

GRAND-SIMON.

I'd like to speak to him.

DORINE.

On whose behalf?

GRAND-SIMON.

My own.

DORINE.

Who are you?

GRAND-SIMON.

I'm someone whom you do not know.

DORINE.

I know that! Does Dr. Mirobolan know you?

GRAND-SIMON.

No, nor I, him.

CRISPIN *gravely*.

What is it?

DORINE.

It's this gentleman, who would like to speak to you.

CRISPIN.

Lead him in, and make it quick.

GRAND-SIMON *after some bows*.

Sir, people have told me that you were a great doctor, especially in divination.[21] So, you see, after having found this out, I made up my mind to come speak to you about a little matter.

CRISPIN.

Speak concisely.

GRAND-SIMON.

You see I love a girl in our village, and there's a certain strange man who goes to her house sometimes. I'd like to find out from you if she loves me like she says, and if I'll marry her because, to tell you the truth, I'm doubtful.

---

[21] Divination is the art of foretelling future events.

CRISPIN.

What does she look like?

GRAND-SIMON.

She's tall, is a brunette, and has a pug nose.

CRISPIN.

Tall, brunette, pug nose?

GRAND-SIMON.

Yes, sir.

CRISPIN.

Take some pills.

GRAND-SIMON.

Some pills?

CRISPIN.

Yes.

GRAND-SIMON.

Some pills?

CRISPIN.

Yes, some pills that you can easily get at the pharmacy. You must take ten, due to your size.

GRAND-SIMON.

But it seems to me that pills are good only for purging people, and not for... .

CRISPIN.

Go! Do what I tell you, and I'll do the rest. It's a science that you do not understand. If you were educated, and if you knew Latin, I'd have you see such things... .

GRAND-SIMON.

Sir, I know Latin because I'm the magistrate of our village.

CRISPIN.

You know Latin?

GRAND-SIMON.

Yes, Sir.

CRISPIN.

Well, so much the better for you. Some other time, do what I tell you, and goodbye! I have business elsewhere.

GRAND-SIMON.

Before leaving, I must pay you.

CRISPIN.

That's a good idea.

GRAND-SIMON *digging through his pocket.*

Some pills!

CRISPIN *holding out his hand.*

Yes, some pills! Quickly, quickly, and goodbye.

GRAND-SIMON.

Here is a gold coin. If this works… .

CRISPIN.

I understand, that's enough.

GRAND-SIMON *aside.*

These erudite men are always so abrupt! Good day, sir.

CRISPIN.

Your servant.

He leaves.

DORINE *having closed the door.*

A gold coin and a silver coin, in so little time! I made you a doctor, you should give me half of it.

CRISPIN.

Dorine, leave me alone! We'll have a feast together, but, for the moment, …

More knocking on the door.

DORINE.

Someone's knocking on the door. This is a lot of practical experience.

CRISPIN.

By God, I'm growing tired. Ah, it's the devil himself.

SCENE IX.

MIROBOLAN, DORINE, CRISPIN

MIROBOLAN.

Dorine, have you been thinking... .

DORINE.

Sir, I just put the cadaver in the cellar, and here's one of your colleagues, who having learned that you were performing a dissection, has come to watch you.

MIROBOLAN *after several bows.*

Sir, although I do not have the honor of knowing you, you are always welcome here, but I will not start work until tomorrow. If you would do me a favor, you could listen to a little speech that, I believe, will not be common place.

CRISPIN.

Ah, sir! I wouldn't miss it. The reputation of Dr. Mirobolan is a reputation which… in these matters… is indeed… I wouldn't miss it.

DORINE.

Sir, if you want me to prepare this room, you must give me the opportunity.

MIROBOLAN.

Later! Sir, I would like to ask you for opinion about a patient whom I am treating.

CRISPIN.

Sir, you'll excuse me, please! I have to take care of some urgent business.

MIROBOLAN.

I will be brief. You see this patient had a quatrain fever,[22] tertian[23] and continual.[24] We have broken the fever.

---

[22] Quatrain fever is a fever that usually has a seventy-two-hour-life cycle and often results from dehydration. This often causes even more dehydration.

[23] Tertian fever has a forty-eight-hour life cycle.

[24] The patient is suffering from malaria.

MIROBOLAN (continued)

However, there is something which worries me about him, besides severe insomnia, which greatly fatigues him. What he spits up is extremely white, and, in my opinion, is a very bad sign because a *pituita alba, aqua inter cutem supervenit*,[25] as Hippocrates tells us. It is as you know what the Greeks call Leucophegmatia.[26] According to Hippocrates, the white spittle is an obvious sign that edema[27] will follow. What do you think is the best thing to give him to prevent this?

CRISPIN.

You don't need any advice. You're a man who…. . yes…. . in fact I can't say anything.

MIROBOLAN.

No, speak frankly! I will be put at ease to know your opinion about it.

CRISPIN.

I'm far from knowing much…. .

---

[25] With the coughing of white phlegm, liquid fills the tissues.

[26] Leucophegmatia is when the body has an excess of white corpuscles. This results in the enlargement of the spleen and the lymph glands.

[27] Edema is the excessive accumulation of serous fluid in the tissues.

MIROBOLAN.

As for me, I act without pretense. I am not one of those gentlemen who cherish only his own opinion, and who would stick to it, and allow a patient to die. Speak, I will listen to you.

DORINE *low to Crispin.*

Say what you can. (*aloud to Mirobolan.*) But sir, hurry up, I have a lot to do.

MIROBOLAN.

Dorine, in just a moment.

CRISPIN.

Sir, with these types of illnesses, I don't know if…. when…. about that…. we….

the….

MIROBOLAN.

Huh?

CRISPIN.

Some pills….

MIROBOLAN.

To give him some pills would be to ruin his constitution, which is already very altered by the chaos caused his other infirmities.

CRISPIN.

Oh, I wasn't saying that. I was saying that the pills that I took this morning oblige me to leave immediately.

MIROBOLAN.

Oh, I do not wish to keep you. Dorine, direct the gentleman where he needs to go. I am your servant.

CRISPIN *getting undressed.*

I'm going to wait for you without any more discussion.

DORINE.

I'm going to hurry and get a reply, and think at the same time how to deal with things so that when the real hanged man is brought in, no one will notice the difference.

End of second Act.

ACT III.

FIRST SCENE.

GERALDE, CRISPIN

CRISPIN.

Well, sir, what do you have to say about my adventure?

GERALDE.

I would say that it is peculiar.

CRISPIN.

Hanged man, doctor, twine, lancets, nails, pills! By God, it's just too much.

GERALDE.

That is true! It was a lot to deal with, but you must return to Dr. Mirobolan's house.

CRISPIN.

Me, sir?

GERALDE.

Yes, you.

CRISPIN.

By God, I don't want to go back to have myself sliced open or to get beaten with a stick. You could go yourself.

GERALDE.

It is true that I could, but I fear, by going there, that I might ruin my love affair because if Dr. Mirobolan bumps into me, he will not fail to inform my father about what is happening. As for you, you risk nothing. He does not know you.

CRISPIN.

I risk my back, my arms, my legs, my body! From the way that I heard Dr. Mirobolan speak: nails, twine, lancets, a doctor has no more pity on a man than a lawyer has on a gold coin.

GERALDE.

It is, nevertheless, necessary my dear Crispin to return once again. And, you must believe that when I can, I will recognize all of your services that you have given me.

CRISPIN.

Oh, I don't doubt it, but at least tell me the reason that I must return.

GERALDE.

Here, listen to the letter that you brought to me.

I have many things to tell you, but I do not have the time to write them. Just to find the time for this note, I had to employ several stratagems. Send Crispin as soon as possible. I will do everything in my power to give him a letter, which will instruct you about everything. If I can manage to talk with you in person, believe that I will do so with great joy. Goodbye, love me as I love you, and rest assured that I will never marry anyone else but you. ALCINE.

Well, you see, Crispin... .

CRISPIN.

Yes, I see that I must go back there. But, if Dr. Mirobolan, who's taken me for a hanged man in my own clothes and has seen me in a doctor's robe, should recognize me, how do I get out of it without a beating? Huh?

GERALDE.

It is true that that would be very awkward, but, my dear Crispin, you must risk something for your master. Think! Devise something so that you run no risk.

CRISPIN.

Listen! Get me a doctor's robe! I'd rather appear before him that way than like a hanged man. As for the rest, I'll get out of it the best that I can. I was almost caught by the pills. I will escape by some other remedy.

GERALDE.

I will go on that note to the second-hand clothing store and pick up what you need. Anyway, go to my father's house to get the money that he promised you because it is possible that we will really need it.

CRISPIN.

I'm going. But sir, teach me in Latin: I'm a doctor.

GERALDE.

Gladly: MEDICUS SUM.

CRISPIN.

MEDICUS SUM, MEDICUS SUM?

GERALDE.

Very good.

CRISPIN.

Enough, goodbye. Go! Think about the robe, and I'm going to the old man's house. MEDICUS SUM, MEDICUS SUM. What a wonderful thing to know Latin. I must repeat these words often for fear of forgetting them: MEDICUS SUM, MEDICUS SUM. That's enough. Let's go to Mr. Lisidor's. But, I see him coming.

SCENE II.

LISIDOR, CRISPIN, MARIN

LISIDOR.

What are you doing here?

CRISPIN.

Sir, I got bored at the house. I took a walk.

LISIDOR.

Where is your master? Tell me.

CRISPIN.

What an excellent question! He's at Bourges. Would you be so kind as to give me the money so I can go back?

LISIDOR.

Oh yeah. Tell me, where does he room in Bourges?

CRISPIN.

He lives near the university.

LISIDOR.

What is the name of the street?

CRISPIN.

The street?

LISIDOR.

Yes.

CRISPIN.

It is called…. . It is called…. . You were there before me, you know it well.

LISIDOR.

Nevertheless?

CRISPIN.

I can't remember anymore. There're so many darn names in that town, which are difficult to retain, and then I don't know how to get them into my head, and I hardly worry about them. What's the point of dealing with all of these damn names? When one's housed, one's housed.

MARIN.

He's quite right.

CRISPIN.

Damn it, shut up, or…. . Do you see… damn! Now… .

LISIDOR.

Patience… .

CRISPIN.

I just don't want him to meddle in something which is none of his business.

LISIDOR.

Shut up! What does your master do most of the time?

CRISPIN.

He studies, and then he often dines or has late night suppers with people who speak Latin like devils. What I find amusing is that they argue as if they wanted to strangle each other, and the whites of their eyes show. Afterwards, they quiet down by quaffing five or six draughts.

LISIDOR.

That is not bad. But, three or four people have told me that he was in this town, and that they have seen him here.

CRISPIN.

Whoever said that has lied, and I'll support him before all of France.

LISIDOR.

Confess the truth. I will speak of it no more. Is he here?

CRISPIN.

I'll confess nothing because it's not true.

LISIDOR.

Oh, I know otherwise, and if you continue to pretend… .

CRISPIN.

Do you want to make me say something which isn't true?

LISIDOR.

Therefore, I lied?

CRISPIN.

You have all that you wish, but it isn't true. It isn't true.

MARIN.

Sir, leave this insolent man. He'll make you angry for no reason.

CRISPIN.

Insolent! Damn, you liar! I'm going to have to beat you up and down.

They start to fight.

MARIN.

Come on! Come on! I'll rearrange you.

LISIDOR *separating them with his cane.*

Scoundrels, if you do not stop, I will give you a hundred blows with my cane. Ah damn, this is too much. Crispin, since your master is not in Paris, I order you to go to Bourges and to tell him that once he lets me know his address, I will send him some money via bank check in that town.

CRISPIN.

But, sir…

LISIDOR.

No more responses! Do not come near my house if you do not want a hundred blows from my cane.

CRISPIN.

If you beat me, I know what I'll do.

LISIDOR.

What will you do?

CRISPIN *pointing to Marin.*

I'll beat the devil out of him.

LISIDOR.

Why will you beat him?

CRISPIN.

Well, why would you beat me?

LISIDOR.

Because you are a scoundrel.

CRISPIN.

And since he's a scum. and he wants me beaten.

LISIDOR *raising his cane.*

I will give you... .

CRISPIN.

Go ahead and strike, you'll see if I don't respond to it.

LISIDOR.

Ah, my God, I cannot suffer anymore of this.

Lisidor attempts to hit Crispin with his cane. Crispin lowers his head, which causes Lisidor to fall, and Crispin strikes Marin with his fist, who falls to the other side, and Crispin runs off.

SCENE III.

LISIDOR, MARIN

MARIN.

Ah, the traitor! I believe that he maimed me with that that blow.

LISIDOR.

Marin, come help me get up.

MARIN.

But, sir, I need someone to help me up.

Noël Le Breton de Hauteroche

LISIDOR *getting up, aided by Marin.*

The scoundrel! He will pay for that.

MARIN.

If I ever catch him, he'll be sorry.

LISIDOR.

I hurt my shoulder in the fall.

MARIN.

And I believe that I have a dislocated jaw.

LISIDOR.

He gave you quite a blow.

MARIN.

With all of his strength.

LISIDOR.

Patience.

MARIN.

I have to be despite myself.

LISIDOR.

Go see if Dr. Mirobolan is at home.

MARIN.

What, sir? You want to talk to him again about your marriage, even after his wife has told you to your face that it'll never happen.

LISIDOR.

No matter, I want to try again.

MARIN.

Very good! That's to say that you want to be refused once again and that you derive pleasure from hearing them sing your praises while rubbing you the wrong way.

LISIDOR.

I admit to you frankly that I expect the refusal, and that, at the same time, I am even consoled, but I want the pleasure of stating the fact to Dr. Mirobolan and letting him know that I will never think of him other than as a man who lets himself be led around by the nose like a fool.

MARIN.

But what purpose will that serve you?

LISIDOR.

Just do what I say. See if he is at home.

SCENE IV.

DORINE, LISIDOR, MARIN

MARIN *knocking on Mirobolan's door.*

Hello!

DORINE.

Who is it?

MARIN.

Is Dr. Mirobolan here?

DORINE.

No. Who is asking for him?

LISIDOR.

It is I, my dear.

DORINE.

He's not here. Do you want to speak to madam? She's upstairs asleep. I'll go wake her.

LISIDOR.

You must let her sleep. My dear child, if you could, with care, get her to consent to give me Alcine in marriage, I would... .

DORINE.

Give you Alcine in marriage! By Jove, what could you do with her, at your age?

LISIDOR.

Well, I would… .

DORINE.

My word, whatever you would do would be worthless. But, do you have anything else to say to me? I'm going back in the house.

LISIDOR.

My dear, tell Dr. Mirobolan that his friend Lisidor came to see him, and that I pray that he think about what he promised me. Goodbye, my good child.

DORINE.

Goodbye, sir, I'll not miss you.

Is that old man crazy imagining marrying an eighteen-year-old girl? One must admit that when the elderly get love on their mind, they're a hundred times more extravagant than the young.

SCENE V.

CRISPIN *dressed as Doctor*, DORINE

CRISPIN *entering.*

At home… at home, I tell you. I'll reply to you soon.

DORINE.

What's wrong, Crispin? And why are you dressed that way?

CRISPIN.

Two people that I met told me that they were studying medicine, and asked me my opinion about trans…. the… there…. there…. transconfusion of blood. They insisted that I speak to the point of exhaustion.

DORINE.

What did they tell you?

CRISPIN.

How in the devil should I know? One beast on another…. The artery…. The literal blood…. arterial…. An artery from which blood enters…. A dead animal, the other which is not better off. The bad blood spilling out…. The good in the veins of the other beast…. Now, the devil take them away with all of their reasoning.

DORINE.

You should've prescribed them pills.

CRISPIN.

I would have with all my heart, but they each had fifty in their belly.

DORINE *laughing*.

But why do you have that outfit?

CRISPIN.

I'm wearing it to have access to your home, and to... .

SCENE VI.

LISIDOR, MARIN, CRISPIN, DORINE

LISIDOR *returning*.

My dear Dorine, I forgot to give you this ring, but I want to recover... .

CRISPIN *turning away*.

Ah!

MARIN.

Sir, if I'm not mistaken, there's Crispin dressed in a long robe.

LISIDOR.

What are you doing here in that outfit?

CRISPIN *gravely*.

What do you want from me? Do you have some secret illness? Speak, in the absence of Dr. Mirobolan, I can give you good advice.

LISIDOR.

No, scoundrel, we have no illness.

CRISPIN.

Scoundrel!

LISIDOR.

Yes, scoundrel.

CRISPIN.

NON SUM COQUINUS, MEDICUS SUM, MEDICUS SUM.

LISIDOR.

You, a doctor!

CRISPIN.

Yes, a doctor, and you're an insolent man. ARACA, LOSTOVI, BARITONOVAI, FORLUTUM, TRANSCONFUSIONA…. If you were reasonable, I'd speak to you about transconfusion, but I see what your problem is. Go! Take some pills.

LISIDOR.

If I get a stick, I will give you a hundred blows.

CRISPIN.

That would go against my prescription.

DORINE.

Sir, come in the house to wait for our master, and leave those eccentric men behind.

CRISPIN *entering the house with Dorine.*

You're right. That's a good idea.

MARIN.

Sir, I doubt that that was Crispin because he speaks Latin.

LISIDOR.

It is undoubtedly he. I suspect some ruse, and I want to go in and find out what it is.

He knocks on the door.

DORINE.

What do you need, sir? Do you want to continue quarreling with that honest man who's in our home?

LISIDOR.

He is a scoundrel of a valet.

DORINE.

That's not true. He's one of our master's colleagues, and you have bad grace to speak of him in that manner. I'll complain about this as soon as... .

SCENE VII.

MIROBOLAN, LISIDOR, DORINE, MARIN

MIROBOLAN *entering.*

I tell you that that is not possible, and that that opinion is bizarre.

LISIDOR.

Sir... .

MIROBOLAN.

You must have shallow thoughts to imagine a thing so far from common sense.

LISIDOR.

Sir, I want… .

MIROBOLAN.

There is no doubt that this idea came from a man who had a high fever.

DORINE.

What's the matter, sir, that causes you to get carried away like this?

MIROBOLAN.

Some people have an opinion about transfusion which is absurd.

DORINE.

They are crazy… .

MIROBOLAN.

No doubt.

LISIDOR.

They are not right because it was publically outlawed. You know… .

SCENE VIII.

LISE, MIROBOLAN, DORINE, LISIDOR, MARIN

LISE *to Dorine.*

Is Dr. Mirobolan here?

DORINE.

There he is. She came just in time.

MIROBOLAN.

What do you want of me?

LISE.

I want you hanged! Having prescribed pills to me that made me feel like I was dying.

MIROBOLAN.

Me?

LISE.

Yes, you. Look at you, great deceivers. You often prescribe things that are wrong and all over the place. Let's go, take them, and see what happens to you. Pills to find a lost dog!

MIROBOLAN.

You are mistaken, I have never seen you.

LISE.

Never! Did I not recently give you a silver coin?

MIROBOLAN.

You are crazy.

LISE.

You're lying, and… .

SCENE IX.

GRAND-SIMON, LISE, MIROBOLAN, LISIDOR, DORINE, MARIN

GRAND-SIMON.

Ah! If I see this Dr. Mirobolan, I'm going to tell everybody about his swindling of people.

LISE.

Hold on, there he is.

GRAND-SIMON.

By God, sir, you must be a complete fool to prescribe pills to find out if one is loved by a woman. And me fool enough to take them! They almost sent me to the next world, and I haven't come back yet.

MIROBOLAN.

You are crazy to speak to me like that. I do not know you at all.

GRAND-SIMON.

Did I not just give you a gold coin?

LISE.

He'll deny everything to you, just like he did with me.

MIROBOLAN.

Both of you should be put in an asylum because you are crazy.

GRAND-SIMON.

Damn! You're lying. I'm not crazy. Stop this nonsense because I'll give you a whack with my stick on your ears.

LISE.

And I'll pull out your beard.

MIROBOLAN.

Ah! This is too much to bear. Dorine, go find the police superintendent.

GRAND-SIMON.

Let her go! Let her go! I'll wait for him.

LISE.

And me too.

GRAND-SIMON.

You'll see how these gentlemen kill people, and they're always right. By God, I want my gold coin back.

DORINE.

My word, if you're not quiet, I'm going for the police superintendent.

GRAND-SIMON.

That's what I'm asking for.

LISE.

And that's what I'm waiting for.

SCENE X.

FELIANTE, CRISPIN, LISIDOR, MIROBOLAN,
DORINE, MARIN,
GRAND-SIMON, LISE

CRISPIN.

But, madam… .

FELIANTE.

But, sir, once again, I do not want my daughter speaking to people *tête-à-tête*. If you want to see my husband, you can come when he is at home.

CRISPIN.

Madam, can you believe that... .

FELIANTE.

I know what to believe, but, once again, you cannot come in when my husband is not home.

LISE *to Simon.*

It seems to me that that face strongly resembles that of the doctor who prescribed pills for me.

GRAND-SIMON.

By God, it's the doctor who made me feel like dying. Ah deceiver! You'll give me back my money.

LISE.

You'll return mine too.

LISIDOR *taking him by the collar.*

Ah, scoundrel! I have got you now.

CRISPIN.

NON SUM ROGUS. MEDICUS SUM.

MIROBOLAN.

Gentlemen, you must not mistreat one of my colleagues like that. One must at least allow him to explain his logic.

LISIDOR.

He's my son's valet.

LISE.

He's the doctor who prescribed pills for us.

GRAND-SIMON.

And which have given me a great deal of pain.

LISIDOR.

Scoundrel! Answer these charges.

CRISPIN.

Sir, I must no longer hide anything from you. Your son has never left Paris because of the love that he has for Dr. Mirobolan's daughter. She loves him passionately, and they love each other and made me play several characters to help them in their relationship.

FELIANTE.

My daughter loves your master?

CRISPIN.

Yes, madam, and ardently.

FELIANTE.

As for the son, it is something, but as for the father, he must never hope to marry my daughter.

GRAND-SIMON.

But what made you tell us to take pills? How could that help your master's relationship?

CRISPIN.

Those are matters which I'll explain at another time.

MIROBOLAN.

You see how you blamed me without cause. Be good enough to come back another time, I promise to satisfy you in one way or another.

LISE.

I agree, but don't fail.

GRAND-SIMON.

I agree, too, but no more pills.

MIROBOLAN.

No more pills. Goodbye.

LISIDOR.

Your master, you say, passionately loves Dr. Mirobolan's daughter?

CRISPIN.

Yes, sir, and a hundred times more than I told you.

LISIDOR.

Well, if that is the case, I see that it is necessary to consent to his marriage to her, provided that the father and the mother also consent.

MIROBOLAN.

As for me, I wish it with all my heart, provided that my wife wishes it.

FELIANTE.

I do not really know if I should wish it.

MIROBOLAN.

But, my wife... .

FELIANTE

Since you beg me, I will agree.

LISIDOR.

Where is your master?

CRISPIN.

I see him coming just in time.

Noël Le Breton de Hauteroche

LAST SCENE.

GERALDE, MIROBOLAN, FELIANTE, LISIDOR, DORINE, CRISPIN, MARIN

LISIDOR.

Come, gentleman from Bourges.

GERALDE *throwing himself at his father's knees.*

Ah my father! I ask for your forgiveness.

MIROBOLAN.

Good Lord! Let's leave this discussion. Let's go in the house, and talk about it all.

FELIANTE.

That is a good idea. Come on. Let's go in.

MIROBOLAN.

Let's go in, Mr. Lisidor. The honor belongs to you.

LISIDOR.

Since you wish, let's go in.

They go in.

CRISPIN.

Marin?

MARIN.

What do you want?

CRISPIN.

With everything today, I succeeded. I'm going in. I'm going in by Jove. I'm going in too.

THE END.

Noël Le Breton de Hauteroche

CHRONOLOGY OF HAUTEROCHE'S LIFE

1617 ?

This is the probable year of the birth of Noël Le Breton, son of Noël I Le Breton (1598 ?-1678), "boutonnier," and the mother not subsequently identified (?-1642).

1635-1637 ?

Hauteroche leaves Paris, with a view to a career in the army in Valencia, Spain.

He joins a French acting troupe in Valladolid.

1638-?

He directs a troupe of French actors in Germany and travels with them there.

The date of their return cannot be surmised.

1650

He becomes the director of a provincial troupe that includes Catherine Desurlis, then her sisters Madeleine (1652) and Estiennette (1653). His friendship with their father Étienne Desurlis would predate their association with the troupe.

1654

Scarron creates the stock character Crispin in his comedy *L'Écolier de Salamanque.*

April 1

The "acte of association d'une troupe de comédiens de campagne sous la direction de Noël Breton, sieur de Hauteroche" is signed.

The "promesse faite par la troupe de Noël Breton, sieur de Hauteroche à Cathérine de Surlis" is signed. This is the earliest act of constitution of the troupe, for one year, co-signed by Jannequin ("Rochefort"), François de la Court, Jehan Loseu ("Beauchaisne"), Drouyn, François Serdin, and Estiennette Desurlis.

September 29

At Fontenay-le-Comte, Hauteroche becomes the godfather to the son of Claude Jannequin and Madeleine Desurlis; His troupe entertains.

1655

April

Hauteroche, now permanently with the stage name, becomes a member of the Théâtre du Marais.

He remains only for the 1655-1656 season, after which the company loses its lease. The Théâtre du Marais closes from April 1657 to March 31, 1659.

Summer

He acts himself in Quinault's comedy *La Comédie sans comédie.*

1657

April

He and the members of his troupe leave Paris to act in the provinces. The exact date of their return is not known but may be within the year.

1658-59

Floridor, director of the Théâtre de l'Hôtel de Bourgogne takes on Hauteroche, as a replacement for Pierre Lazard who died in 1657.

Hauteroche's first season corresponds with Molière's return from the provinces.

1660

Molière creates *Sganarelle ou le cocu imaginaire*.

March

Hauteroche's signature appears on the rental agreement of the Hôtel de Bourgogne.

1662

He creates the lead rôle of Baron de la Crasse in Raymond Poisson's comedy *Le Baron de la Crasse*.

He plays Pompée in Pierre Corneille's *Sertorius*.

Molière creates *L'École des femmes*.

Noël Le Breton de Hauteroche

1663

Molière creates *L'Impromptu de Versailles*, which includes a caricature of Hauteroche's tragic diction in the rôle of Pompée.

Hauteroche unofficially assumes on occasion Floridor's function as the troupe's *orateur.*

March 3

Hauteroche, with the other actors, signs a four-year rental agreement on the Hôtel de Bourgogne.

1664

Fifteen lyric poems by Hauteroche appear in *Les Delices de la poesie des plus célèbres auteurs du temps*, published by Ribou and dedicated to the duc de Coislin.

Hauteroche's signature appears on la lettre-mémoire of the actors of the Hôtel de Bourgogne concerning pensions.

1665

December 18

He performs the rôle of Éphestion in Jean Racine's *Alexandre le grand.*

1666

January

Hauteroche performs the rôle of Tygrane in Thomas Corneille's *Antiochus*. This opening is a special performance for Louis XIV given by the duc de Créqui.

1667

Hauteroche plays the rôle of Lira, "poète de la cour" in Jean-Baptiste Lully's *Ballet des muses*.

November 19

He creates the rôle of Phénix in Racine's *Andromaque*.

1668

February 18

He plays, along with Brécourt, one of the rôles of *prétendants* in Thomas Corneille's *Laodice, reine de Cappadoce*.

June 9

Raymond Poisson's *Le Poète basque*, in which Hauteroche plays himself, is first performed,.

July 12

Hauteroche's first play is produced, *L'Amant qui ne flatte point* inspired by Molière's *Le Misanthrope* (1666).

November

He creates the rôle of Chicanneau in Racine's comedy *Les Plaideurs*.

1669

L'Amant qui ne flatte point is first published in Paris by Guillain and de Sercy.

He plays the rôle of the "Coadjuteur" in Montfleury's *La Femme juge et partie* in a special performance for the duchesse de Bouillon.

February 2

He creates the rôle of Pompée in abbé Boyer's *Le Jeune Marius*.

February 21

He creates the rôle of Narcisse in Racine's *Britannicus*.

July

Hauteroche's second play *Le Souper mal-apprêté* opens.

1670

Le Souper mal-apprêté is first published in Paris by Guillain and de Sercy.

Crispin médecin is first published by Barbin.

March 22

Hauteroche signs the act of association by which Champmeslé and his wife join the Hôtel de Bourgogne.

April 25

Hauteroche signs a "mémoire" of ratification of the 1,000 livres pension of retired actors from the Hôtel de Bourgogne.

May 10

His third play, *Crispin médecin.* opens.

November 21

He creates the rôle of Paulin in Racine's *Bérénice*.

1671

May 9

He creates the rôle of the lover Hydas in Boyer's *Atalante*.

August

After withdrawal from the theatre of the terminally ill Floridor, Hauteroche takes over directorship of the troupe and the function of *orateur*.

His signature appears on the marriage contract of Claude Deschamps (de Villiers) and Jeanne Guillemain, which is also signed by his future wife Madame J-B Arnauld (Jacqueline Le Sueur) and her mother Radégonde Régnard (née Le Sueur).

Noël Le Breton de Hauteroche

1672

January 5

Hauteroche creates the rôle of Osmin in Racine's *Bajazet*.

August 6

The announcement of Hauteroche's fourth play under the title of *Les Maris infideles ou les apparences trompeuses* is made. However, it was not produced.

November 16

He creates the lead rôle of Théodat in Thomas Corneille's *Théodat*.

November 24

Hauteroche's fifth play, *Le Deuil*, is first performed.

1673

Les Apparence trompeuses and *Le Deuil* are first published in Paris by Promé. *Le Deuil* is headed by a dedication to André Le Camus, chevalier, conseiller ordinaire du roi.

January 13

Hauteroche creates the rôle of Arbate in Racine's *Mithridate*.

January 30

Hauteroche plays in a special performance of *Mithridate* staged as a part of the festivities of the marriage of the duc d'Orléans and Charlotte Elisabeth de Bavière.

August 2

Crispin médecin is played for the duc d'Orléans at his request in a private performance given for him by Monsieur de Boisfranc at Saint-Ouen. Hauteroche is in attendance, playing in a production of *Mithridate*.

1674

July 5

Hauteroche's sixth play, *Crispin musicien*. opens.

September 21

Crispin musicien is first published in Paris by Promé.

1675

Summer

This is the probable first production of his seventh play *Les Nobles de province*.

September 13

His signature appears on the marriage contract of the actor Michel Baron.

1677

January 1

He creates the rôle of Téramène in Racine's *Phèdre*.

1678

Hauteroche's first will and testament is drawn up, his father appears as "legataire universel."

Noël I Le Breton dies.

Le Deuil is performed at Versailles.

January or February

Les Nouvellistes, Hauteroche's eighth play, is first performed. It was not published and is not extant.

August 28

Les Nobles de province first published in Lyons by Amaulry, including an "Au lecteur" not subsequently published.

1679

February 15

His signature appears on the marriage contract of Jean Bouillart.

1680

March

Hauteroche's ninth play *La Bassette*, is first performed. It was not published and is not extant.

August 13

Pierre Le Breton, Hauteroche's half-brother, dies.

August 25

The merging of the Hôtel de Bourgogne and the Théâtre du Guénégaud takes place to form the single Parisian theatre known as La Comédie-Française.

Hauteroche plays the rôle of Téramène in the opening performance of Racine's *Phèdre* at La Comédie-Française.

1682

The first collective edition of Hauteroche's plays is published by Adrien Moetjens in The Hague, *Les Pièces de théâtre du sieur de Hauteroche*, containing in order of publication *L'Amant qui ne flatte point*, *Le Souper mal-apprêté*, *Crispin médecin*, *Le Deuil*, *Les Apparences trompeuses*, *Crispin musicien*, and *Les Nobles de province*.

Hauteroche furnishes a loan to Jacqueline Le Sueur of 2,200 livres for the settlement of her mother's estate.

1684

February 22

L'Esprit folet ou la dame invisible. Hauteroche's tenth play is first produced.

March 20

Hauteroche's retirement from the Hôtel de Bourgogne is officially noted by LaGrange, with "demye part à M. Raisin, l'ainé, demye à Mlle Raisin."

April 17

Hauteroche receives power of attorney for all Jacqueline Le Sueur's financial affairs.

June 7 or June 9

Le Cocher, Hauteroche's eleventh play, is first performed.

1685

L'Esprit folet ou la dame invisible and *Le Cocher* are first published in Paris by Ribou. *Le Cocher* has a preface not subsequently published.

June 25

Hauteroche marries Jacqueline Le Sueur. An inventory is drawn up of Jacqueline's house, rue de Beaurepaire, where the couple will reside.

August 7

Le Cocher is performed for Louis XIV at Marly.

December 10

Hauteroche makes the loan of 3,650 livres to J.B. Défant, colonel de dragons.

1686

Hauteroche's twelfth play, *Le Feint Polonois ou la veuve impertinente* is published for the first in Lyons by Plaignard, after a probable public performance in Lyons. The play was not produced in Paris.

1687

This is the probable year of Hauteroche's blindness, from an unknown cause.

January 17

Hauteroche makes the loan of 1,600 livres to Anne Bellinzani, Madame Michel Ferrand.

1688

March 1

Hauteroche's signature appears on the marriage contract of the actor Duparc's son.

1689

March 22

Hauteroche and his wife rent a house on la rue Saint-Sauveur at 720 livres yearly.

1690

July 26-August 7

Les Bourgeoises de qualité, Hauteroche's thirteenth and last play, is produced at La Comédie-Française.

1691

Les Bourgeoises de qualité is published for the first in Paris by the veuve Gontier, who also published the second collective edition of Hauteroche's plays.

Noël Le Breton de Hauteroche

1694

Jacqueline Le Sueur's signature on the quittance for Hauteroche's pension notes his blindness and bad health.

1695

The Hauteroches rent out a house owned at 16, rue de Beaune (at 300 livres).

1696

A third collective edition of Hauteroche's plays is published in Paris by Guillain.

December 1

The Hauteroches sell a house owned in Aubervilliers (4,500 livres).

1697-1705

Hauteroche makes loans of 6,000 livres to Jean Le Roy, Greffier à la 4e Chambre des Enquêtes, and his wife Geneviève Herault, and of 20,000 livres to Louis Gislain, sieur de Belcourt.

1703

A fourth collective edition of Hauteroche's plays published by Ribou, containing in order of publication *Crispin musician*, *Crispin médecin*, *Le Deuil*, *Les Bourgeoises de qualité*, and *L'Esprit folet ou la dame invisible*.

1704

December 13

Hauteroche's second and final will and testament is drawn up. His executor is Louis Gislain, sieur de Belcourt. His sister Marie is "légataire universelle."

1705

January 14

He makes a loan of 48,000 livres to Marie Bonneau, widow of Charles Fortier, sieur de La Hoguette.

1707

July 14

Hauteroche dies in a house on the rue de la March and is buried in the parish church of Saint-Sauveur.

1713

Jacqueline Le Sueur dies and is buried at the parish church of Saint-Suplice.

Her sister Anne-Marie Le Sueur, widow of Louis de Dours is "légataire universel."

Noël Le Breton de Hauteroche

BIBLIOGRAPHY

I. HAUTEROCHE'S DRAMATIC WRITINGS

Hauteroche, Noël Le Breton. *Les Œuvres de Monsieur de Hauteroche*. La Haye: Moetjens, 1683.

___. *Les Œuvres de Monsieur de Hauteroche*. Paris: Veuve de Gontier, 1691.

___. *Les Œuvres de Monsieur de Hauteroche*. Paris: Guillain, 1696.

___. *Les Œuvres de Monsieur de Hauteroche*. Paris: Ribou, 1703.

___. *Les Œuvres de Monsieur de Hauteroche*. 3 volumes. Paris: Ribou, 1736.

___. *Théâtre de Noël le Breton, sieur de Hauteroche*. Paris: Aux Dépens de la Compagnie, 1772.

___. *Théâtre de Hauteroche*. Paris: Touquet, 1821.

___. Chefs-d'œuvre dramatiques de Hauteroche, et Campistron. Paris: J. Didot, 1824.

___. *L'Amant qui ne flatte point*. Paris: Guillain, et C. de Sercy, 1669.

___. *L'Amant qui ne flatte point*. La Haye: Moetjens, 1682.

Hauteroche. *Le Souper mal-apprêté*. Paris: Guillain, 1670.

____. *Le Souper mal apresté*. Paris: Quinet, 1670.

____. *Le Souper mal apresté*. La Haye: Moetjens, 1682.

____. *Le Souper mal-apprêté*. Paris: Didot, 1778.

____. *Crispin médecin*. Paris: Barbin, 1670.

____. *Crispin médecin*. Paris: Ribou, 1680.

____. *Crispin médecin*. La Haye: Moetjens, 1682.

____. *Crispin médecin*. Amsterdam: P. Rotterdam, 1715

____. *Crispin médecin*. Amsterdam: J. Duim, 1738.

____. *Crispin médecin*. Paris: Duchesne, 1774.

____. *Crispin médecin*. Paris: Ribou, 1767.

____. *Crispin médecin*. Paris: Ribou, 1770.

____. *Crispin médecin*. Paris: Ribou, 1777.

____. *Crispin médecin*. Paris: Vente, 1788.

____. *Crispin médecin*. Paris: Brunet, 1789.

____. *Crispin médecin*. Toulouse: Devers, 1793.

____. *Crispin médecin*. Paris: Théâtre de Molière, 1796.

____. *Crispin médecin*. Paris: Fages, 1802.

____. *Crispin médecin*. Paris: Petitot Répertoire du Théâtre françois, 1804.

Hauteroche. *Crispin médecin*. Paris: Répertoire du Théâtre français, 1818.

____. *Crispin médecin*. Paris: Comédie-Française, 1893.

____. *Crispin médecin*. Paris: Tresse et Stock, 1894.

____. *Crispin médecin*. Paris: Stock, 1903.

____. *Krispyn medicyn*. Amsterdam: A. Magnus, 1685.

____. *Krispyn. medicyn*. Amsterdam: P. Rotterdam, 1715.

____. *Krispyn. medicyn*. Amsterdam: I. Duim, 1738.

____. *Crispin Lakei og Doktor*. Copenhagen: Skuespil til Brug for den danske Skueplads, 1787.

____. *Crispin Lakei og Doktor*. Copenhagen: Trykt paa Gydendals Forlag, 1787.

____. *Crispin médecin*. Copenhagen: Skuespiltekster fra Koinediehuset i Lille Gronnegade, 1921.

____. *Crispin médecin*. Les Contemporains de Molière. ed. Fournel. Paris: Firmin Didot, 1866.

____. *Les Apparences trompeuses ou les maris infidèles*. Paris: Promé, 1673.

____. *Les Apparences trompeuses*. La Haye: Moetjens, 1682.

____. *Les Apparences trompeuses*. Paris: Duchesne, 1765.

____. *Le Deuil*. Paris: Promé, 1673.

Hauteroche. *Le Deuil.* Paris: Loyson, 1673

___. *Le Deuil.* Paris: Promé, 1680.

___. *Le Deuil.* Paris: Ribou, 1680.

___. *Le Deuil.* Paris: La Haye: Moetjens, 1682.

___. *Le Deuil.* Paris: Duchesne, 1774.

___. *Le Deuil.* Paris: Petitot Répertoire du théâtre françois, 1804.

___. *Le Deuil.* Paris: Répertoire général du Théâtre français, 1818.

___. *Le Deuil.* Paris: Théâtre du XVIIᵉ siècle. ed. Jacques Truchet. Paris: Gaillimard, 1986.

___. *Le Deuil.* Paris: Le Deuil. Théâtre du XVII" siècle. ed. Jacques Truchet. Paris: Gaillimard, 1986.

___. *Crispin musicien.* Paris: Promé, 1674.

___. *Crispin musicien.* Paris: Ribou, 1680.

___. *Crispin musicien.* Paris: Ribou, 1705.

___. "Crispin musicien." *Les Contemporains de Molière.* ed. Fournel. Paris: Firmin Didot, 1866.

___. *Krispin, muzikant.* Amsterdam: A. Magnus, 1685.

___. *Krispyn. muzikant.* Amsterdam: H. Bosch, 1727.

___. *Krispyn. muzikant.* Amsterdam: I. Duim, 1739.

Hauteroche. *Les Nobles de province*. Lyon: Amaulry, 1678.

____ *Les Nobles de province*. La Haye: Moetjens, 1682.

___. *La Dame invisible*. Paris: Quay des Augustins, 1685. (pirated Ribou printing)

___. *L'Esprit folet ou la dame invisible*. Paris: Ribou, 1685.

___. *L'Esprit folet: ou la dame invisible*. Paris: Ribou, 1698.

___. *L'Esprit folle, ou la dame invisible*. Paris: Gueffier, 1770.

___. *L'Esprit follet, ou la dame invisible*. Paris: Fin du Répertoire du Théâtre français, 1824.

___. *L'Esprit follet. ou la dame invisible*. Paris: Tous les libraires, 1878.

___. *Le Cocher*. Paris: Ribou, 1685.

___. *Le Cocher*. Paris: Quay des Grands Augustins, 1685. (pirated Ribou printing)

___. *Le Cocher*. Paris: Guillain, 1685.

___. *Le Cocher*. Paris: Aux dépens de la compagnie, 1752.

___. *Le Cocher supposé*. Avignon: Chambeau, 1774.

___.*Le Cocher supposé*. Paris: Fages, 1802.

___. *Le Cocher supposé*. Paris: Répertoire général du Théâtre français, 1818.

Hauteroche. *Le Cocher supposé*. Paris: Veuve Dabo, 1823.

____. *Le Feint Polonais ou la veuve impertinente*. Lyon: Plaignard, 1686.

____. *Les Bourgeoises de qualité*. Paris: Veuve Gontier, 1691.

____. *Les Bourgeoises de qualité*. Berlin: Robert Roger, 1692.

II. SECONDARY SOURCES

Adam, Antoine. *Histoire de la littérature française au XVIIe siècle.* 5 volumes. Paris: Domat-Montchrestien, 1948-1956.

Blanc, André. F.C. Dancourt (1661-1725): *La Comédie française à l'heure du Soleil couchant.* Paris: Editions Jean-Michel Place, 1984.

Bonnassies, J. *La Comédie-Française: Histoire administrative 1658-1757.* Paris: Didier, 1874.

Brooks, William, ed. *Le Théâtre et l'opéra vus par les gazetiers Robinet et Laurent (1670-1678).* Tubingen: Biblio 17, 1993.

Calamé, Alexandre. "Hauteroche." *Dizionario critico della letteratura francese.* ed. Franco Simone. Torino: Unione Tipografico-Editrice Torinese, 1972. volume 1.

Campardon, Émile. *Les Comédiens du roi de la troupe française pendant les derniers siècles.* Paris: Champion, 1879.

Castil-Blaze, H. *Molière musicien: notes sur les œuvres de cet illustre maitre et sur les drames de Corneille, Racine. Quinault. Rancart. Montluc. Maillv, Hauteroche, Saint-Evremont. Dufresny, Palaprat. Dancourt. Lesage, Destouches. J.J. Rousseau. Beaumarchais. etc.; ou se mêlent des considérations sur l'harmonie de la langue française.* 2 volumes. Paris: Castil-Blaze, 1876.

Chevalley, Silvie, *Album Théâtre classique: la vie théâtrale sous Louis XIII et Louis XIV.* Paris: Gallimard-Pléiade, 1970.

Christout, Marie-Françoise. *Le Ballet de Cour de Louis XIV, 1643-1672*. Paris: Editions A. et J. Picard, 1967.

Corneille, Pierre. *Théâtre complet.* ed. Alain Niderst. 3 volumes. Rouen: L'Université de Rouen, 1985.

Curtis, A. Ross. *Crispin 1er: La vie et l'œuvre de Raymond Poisson comédien-poète du XVIIe siècle.* Toronto: University of Toronto Romance Serie 19, 1972.

Dancourt, Florent Carton. *La Comédie de Dancourt 1685-1714.* Paris: G. Charpentier, 1882.

Deierkauf-Holsboer, S. Wilma. *L'Histoire de la mise en scène dans le théâtre français à Paris. Paris:* A.G. Nizet, 1960.

____. *Le Théâtre de Bourgogne.* Paris: A.G. Nizet, 1970. volume 2.

____. *Le Théâtre du Marais.* Paris: A.G. Nizet, 1958. volume 2.

Donneau de Visé, Jean. *Trois comédies.* Paris: Librairie E. Droz, 1940.

DuFail, Noël. *Contes et discours d'Eutrapel.* 2 volumes. Rpt. D. Jouaust. Paris: Librairie des Bibliophiles, 1875.

Émelina, Jean. *Les Valets et les servantes dans le théâtre comique en France de 1610 à 1700.* Grenoble: P.U.G., 1975.

Fournel, Victor. *Les Contemporains de Molière: recueil de comédie, rares ou peu connues jouées de 1650 à 1680 avec l'histoire de chaque théâtre, des notes et notices biographiques.* 2 volumes. Paris: Firmin Didot, 1866.

Doctor Crispin

Fournel. *Le Théâtre au XVIIe siècle: la comédie. Paris*: Lecène, Oudin, et Cie, 1892.

Geoffroy, Julien. "Hauteroche, Crispin médecin." *Cours de littérature dramatique ou, recueil par ordre de matières des feuilletons.* 2e édition. Paris: P.Blanchard, 1825. volume 2.

Isley, Edwin L. *Noël Le Breton de Hauteroche: Seventeenth-century Comic Playwright and Actor.* Ann Arbor, Michigan: *University Microfilms International*, 1998.

Jal, Auguste. "Hauteroche." *Dictionnaire critique de biographie et d'histoire: errata et supplément pour tous les dictionnaires historiques d'après des documents authentiques inédits.* 2e éd. Paris: Plon, 1872.

Joannides, A. *La Comédie-Française de 1680 à 1920: Tableau des représentations.* Paris: Plon, 1921.

Karsh, Mariel O'Neill. "Etat présent des études sur la vie de Noël Le Breton, sieur de Hauteroche (1617-1707), comédien dramaturge, suivi de l'inventaire de ses meubles en 1685." *XVIIe siècle.* 1972.

Knutson, Harold. *Molière: An Archetypal Approach.* Toronto: University of Toronto Press, 1976.

Lachèvre, Frédéric. "Hauteroche." *Dictionnaire des recueils collectifs de poésies publiés de 1597 à 1700.* Paris: H. Leclerc, volume 3. 1904.

LaGrange, Charles Varlet. *Le Registre de La Grange 1659-1685.* eds. Bert, Edward, and Young. Rpt. 2 volumes. Geneva: Librairie E. Droz, 1947.

LaHarpe, Jean-François. *Cours de littérature ancienne et moderne*. Paris: Dupont. 1818. volume 6.

Lancaster, Henry Carrington. *French Dramatic Literature in the Seventeenth Century*. 9 volumes. Baltimore: Johns Hopkins, 1929-1942.

___. *Sunset: A History of Parisian Drama in the Last Years of Louis XIV (1701-1715)*. Baltimore: Johns Hopkins Press, 1945.

___. *Actors/Rôles at the Comédie-Française According to the Répertoire des comédies françaises qui se peuvent jouées en 1685*. Baltimore: Johns Hopkins, 1951.

___. *The Comédie-Française 1680-1701: Plays. Actors, Spectators, Finances*. Baltimore: Johns Hopkins Press, 1941.

___. *The Comédie-Française 1701-1774: Plays. Actors, Spectators*, Finances. Philadelphia: The American Philosophical Society, 1951.

LaPorte, Joseph. "Théâtre de Hauteroche." *Observateur littéraire*. 1760.

Léris, Antoine. "Hauteroche." *Dictionnaire portatif des théâtres, contenant l'origine des différents théâtres de Paris*. C.A. Jambert. 1754.

Mahelot, Laurent. *Le Mémoire de Mahelot. P. Laurent et d'autre décorateurs de l'Hôtel de Bourgogne et de la Comédie- Française au XVII'' siècle*, ed. H.C. Lancaster. Paris: Champion, 1910.

Mélèse, Pierre. *Répertoire analytique des documents contemporains d'information et de critique concernant le théâtre a Paris sous Louis XIV--1659-1715*. Paris: Librairie E. Droz, 1934.

Mercure galant. mai, juin, juillet, aout, 1672; octobre, 1677; Janvier, 1678; février, 1684.

Molière, Jean-Baptiste Poquelin. *Œuvres*. eds. Eugene Despois, Paul Mesnard, and Arthur Desfeuillons. 9 volumes. Paris: Hachette, 1873-1900. volume 3.

___. *Œuvres complètes de Molière*. ed. René Bray. 3 volumes. Paris: Club du meilleur livre, 1954.

Mongrédien, Georges. "Chronologie des troupes qui ont joué à l'Hôtel de Bourgogne (1598-1680)." *Revue d'histoire du théâtre. I-II, (1953)*, pp. 160-74.

Ouville, Antoine Le Métel. *L'Esprit folet*. Paris: Toussaint Quinet, 1642. Pascal, B. Pensées. ed. Louis Lafuma. Paris: Edition du Seuil, 1962.

Parfaict, François and Claude. *Histoire du théâtre françois*. Paris: P.G. Le Mercier Imprimeur-Libraire, 1745. volumes 10-13.

Poisson, Raymond. *Les Œuvres complètes de Raymond Poisson*. Paris: J. Ribou, 1678.

___. *Le Baron de la Crasse et L'Après-soupé des auberges*. ed. Charles Mazouer. Paris: Nizet. 1987.

Quérard, Joseph-Marie. "Hauteroche." *La France littéraire ou dictionnaire bibliographique des savants, historiens et gens de lettres de la France, ainsi que des littérateurs estrangers qui ont écrit en français. Plus particulièrement pendant les XVIIIe et XIXe siècles.* Paris: Firmin Didot, 1830. volume 4.

Quinault, Philippe. *Théâtre choisi.* Paris: Laplace, Sanchez, et Cie, 1882.

Racine, Jean. *Œuvres complètes.* ed. Pierre Clarac. Paris: Le Seuil-l'Integrale, 1962.

Rothchild, James de, ed. *Les Continuateurs de Loret: Lettres en vers de La Gravette de Mayolas,*

Robinet, Boursault Perdou de Subliany, Laurent, et autres (1665-1689). eds. Baron James de

Rothchild and Emile Picot. 3 volumes. Paris: Rahir et Cla. 1899.

Scarron, Paul. *Œuvres de Scarron.* 7 volumes. Paris: Chez Jean François Bastien, 1786.

Sevais, Paul, ed. *Inventaires après-décès et ventes de meubles; Rapports à une histoire de la vie économique et quotidienne du XIVe-XIXe siècles.* Louvain-la-Neuve: Academia, 1988.

III. SUGGESTED READINGS

Abraham, Claude. *On the Structure of Molière's Comédies-Ballets*. Paris: Biblio 17, 1984.

Antoine, André. *Le Théâtre*. Paris: Les Editions de France, 1932.

Bluche, François. *Louis XIV*. Paris: Fayard, 1986.

Brereton, Geoffrey. *French Comic Drama from the Sixteenth to the Eighteenth Century*. London: Methuen, 1977.

Calderón de la Barca, Pedro. *Primera Parte de Comedias de Don Pedro Claderón de la Barca*. ed. A. Valbuena Briones. Madrid: Clasicos Hispanicos, 1974. volume 1.

___. *Select Plays of Calderón*. ed. Norman Maccoll. New York: Macmillan, 1888.

Curtis, A. Ross. "Le Valet Crispin et le premier grand interprète du rôle au XVIIe siècle." *Romanisch Forschunaen*. volume 78. Fasc 2/3. 1966.

Despois, Eugene André. *Le Théâtre français sous Louis XIV*. 3e édition. Paris: Librairie Hachette, 1886.

Forestier, Georges. *Le Théâtre dans le théâtre sur la scène française du XVIIe siècle*. Geneva: Droz, 1981.

Hall, H. Gaston. *Comedy in Context: Essays on Molière*. Jackson, Mississippi: University Press of Mississippi, 1984.

Noël Le Breton de Hauteroche

Hawkins, Frederick. *Annals of the French Stage from its Origin to the Death of Racine.* 2 volumes. New York: Haskell House Publishers, 1970.

Hélard-Cosnier, Colette. "'La Scène est à Paris'... de Calderon à d'Ouville." *Deux siècles de relations hispano-françaises de Commynes a Madame d'Aulnoy: Actes du colloque international du CRECIF.* ed. Daniel-Henri Pageaux. Paris: L'Harmattan, 1987.

Lancaster, Henry Carrington, ed. *Five French Farces.* Baltimore, Maryland: Johns Hopkins Press. 1937.

LaVallière, Louis César de la Baume. *Bibliothèque du théâtre François depuis son origine; contenant un extrait de tous les ouvrages composés pour ce théâtre: depuis les mystères jusqu'aux pièces de Pierre Corneille; une liste chronologique de celles composées depuis cette dernière époque jusqu'à présent; avec deux tables alphabétiques, l'une des auteurs et l'autre des pièces.* Dresde: Michel Groell, 1768.

Lemoine, Jean. *Des Œillets: une grande comédienne, une maitresse de Louis XIV.* Paris: Perrin, 1938.

Lintilhac, Eugène. *Histoire générale du théâtre en France--La Comédie du dix-septième siècle.* Paris: Ernest Flammarion, 1904.

Loliée, Frédéric. *La Comédie-Française: Histoire de la maison de Molière.* Paris: Lucien LaVeur, 1907.

Lough, John. *Paris: Theatre Audiences in the Seventeenth and Eighteenth Centuries.* London: Oxford University Press, 1957.

Martin, Henri-Jean. *Livre, pouvoirs,et société à Paris au XVII" siècle (1598-1701).* 2 volumes. Geneva: Librairie Droz, 1969.

Mélèse, Pierre. *Le Théâtre et son public à Paris sous Louis XIV.* Geneva: Droz, 1934.

Ouville, Antoine Le Métel. *L'Elite des contes du Sieur d'Ouville.* 2 volumes. Rpt. L'Édition de Rouen 1680. Paris: Librairie des Bibliophiles, 1883.

Philipot, Emmanuel. *La Vie et l'œuvre littéraire de Noël DuFail: Gentilhomme Breton.* Paris: Librairie Ancienne Honore Champion, 1914.

Rohde, Karolus. *Noël le Breton. Sieur de Hauteroche. Theil I. Dissertatio Inauguralis Philoaica. OUAM. Consensu et auctbritate. Amplissiini Philosophorum Ordinis in Alma Litterarum Universitate Gryphiswaldensi Ad Summos in Philosophia Honores Rite Capessendos Die XXVII.* Kunike, Gryphiswaldiae: Typis Frid. 1877.

Voos, Wilhelm. *Hauteroche Noël Le Breton (1617-1707) Schauspieler und Lustspieldichter, Inaugural: Dissertation zur Erlangung des Doktormurde einer Hohen Philosophischen Fakultat der Universitat Koln.* Ohligs: Buchdruckerei Carl Bieth, 1927.

Wildenstein, Daniel. *Inventaires après décès d'artistes et de collectionneurs français du XVII", conserves au Minutier central des notaires de la Seine, aux archives nationales.* Paris: Les Beaux-arts, 1967.

About the Translator:

Edwin L. Isley is currently teaching at Wittenberg University. He received his doctorate from The Ohio State University in seventeenth-century French drama and early modern philosophy.

He resides in Columbus Ohio with his wife, two dogs, and two cats.

Dr. Isley intends to publish a translation of all of Hauteroche's eleven published plays as well as his two unpublished plays located in La Bibliothèque Nationale de Paris.

www.ingramcontent.com/pod-product-compliance
Lightning Source LLC
Chambersburg PA
CBHW060938120626
46557CB00003B/1049

* 9 7 8 0 6 9 2 2 3 5 5 0 8 *